Carla Visser

HANDMADE
Personalized
Photo Gifts

Over 75 creative DIY gifts and
keepsakes to make from
your photographs

Carla Visser

Handmade
Personalized
Photo Gifts

Over 75 creative DIY gifts and
keepsakes to make from
your photographs

David and Charles

WINO WA PRINTER
UNAPATIKANA HAPA
KWA BEI NAFSU

Contents

Introduction

Few things in life evoke emotions as strongly as photographs do – capturing those special moments, allowing them to live forever. It's little wonder then that we have this desire to display them wherever possible. In doing so, we can enjoy them more often, bless loved ones with personalized gifts, or create beautiful artwork and fun crafts.

Although I'd never call myself a professional photographer, I've always loved taking photos. I enjoy taking close-ups of fat little baby cheeks and hands, interesting surfaces, and capturing special moments. There's nothing I love more than lying in bed at night, going through the images on my camera, and reliving each moment with a huge, satisfied smile on my face. The sad reality though, is that we don't always actually get round to putting those special moments to print. My hope, therefore, is that this book will inspire you to take your images and use them! I'm going to show you that there's so much more you can do with a photo than simply putting it in a frame. Photos can be edited, transformed, transferred or displayed in new and fun ways.

The inspiration behind this book came while I was teaching a group of eager crafters how to transfer normal laser printed images onto canvas. I was pleasantly surprised by my students' enthusiasm and by the professional-looking results some of them managed to produce. I happened upon this technique while I was desperately looking for the perfect christening gift for a good friend of mine. I wanted to give them a real keepsake, something that truly captured this special event in their lives. I asked them for a few beautiful baby photos, to which I then added some wording and scrapbook elements. I applied the final paper printouts to the canvas using a gel medium, and let it dry overnight. The next morning, while admiring my handiwork, I could not believe how easy it had been to create such a special and unique gift.

After being approached to do a book filled with photo ideas, I was eager to share all of the clever canvas ideas I'd grown to love. But I soon realized that I'd have to expand beyond just canvas. I began experimenting with different techniques and surfaces and was absolutely amazed with the exciting results. It was also often frustrating though, especially when I simply could not get a technique to work. Then I'd scour the Internet looking for possible solutions – always coming to the same conclusion. Sometimes a technique simply won't work with one printer brand or the gel medium of another manufacturer. The key is to follow the instructions as carefully as possible, and, should it be unsuccessful, trying to alternate your medium or printer or sometimes even your surface. Experimentation is the best solution and can be quite fun and rewarding if you approach it with the right attitude.

Most importantly of all though, keep in mind that you are creating a hand-crafted item of which you'll always be proud. Tiny flaws and imperfections might just add to the appeal or create even more interest. I hope you'll be inspired by the projects in this book, get really creative, and fill your life with your special moments.

General information and tips

The book is divided into sections according to the surface on which you will be working. Some of the techniques are the same, regardless of the surface that you use. Here I've included explanations of the various methods and terminology used to avoid repetition throughout some sections of the book.

IMAGES

PHOTOGRAPHS: Standard photos that can be printed at any photo lab. You can print gloss or matte, depending on your preference, and choose various sizes. At some kiosks you can edit your photos, for example, by printing them in sepia or by removing a red-eye effect. Keep in mind that if you print in bulk each print will work out cheaper. Alternatively, use existing or old photographs from your albums at home.

INKJET PRINTS: Most households have an inkjet printer, making this the most convenient method to use. Inkjet printers use ink cartridges, placing extremely small droplets of ink onto paper to create an image. This ink isn't waterproof and might run when it comes into contact with water. Because some projects specifically ask that you use inkjet prints, you'll have to protect these images by coating them with an acrylic spray. Images can be printed onto standard copier paper unless otherwise specified.

LASER PRINTS: Most offices and copier shops use laser printers because although they're expensive to buy, they're much more cost-effective in the long run. These printers come with cartridges filled with a powder, also known as toner, which is applied to the paper using thermal technology. These prints are waterproof and thus ideal for any craft project that requires the use of a 'wet' transfer medium. As with inkjet prints, standard copier paper will suffice.

Photocopiers also use toner-based cartridges, which means you can use a photocopy in any project that asks for a laser printed image.

PHOTOCOPIES: These are a good alternative if you don't want to use your original photographs. You can increase or reduce the size of the image on the copier settings, and make colour or black and white prints. As with laser printed images, the ink is waterproof and won't run if covered in a 'wet' medium.

MIRROR IMAGE PRINTS: Many projects ask for the images to be printed in reverse so that the final transfers will be the right way around. This is especially important if your image has text or numbers on it. Most computers have a version of a Paint program in which you can do this. Alternatively, many printers have the option to select printing mirror/ reverse images.

IMAGE EDITING: There are various readily-available image-editing programmes, for example PICASA, which are available online for free. You can also do some editing in a basic program like Word, especially if you only need to resize or duplicate your image. Nowadays, most cameras come standard with their own photo editing software that you can install. Alternatively, if you're really stuck, email your image to your local copy shop and ask them to help you out.

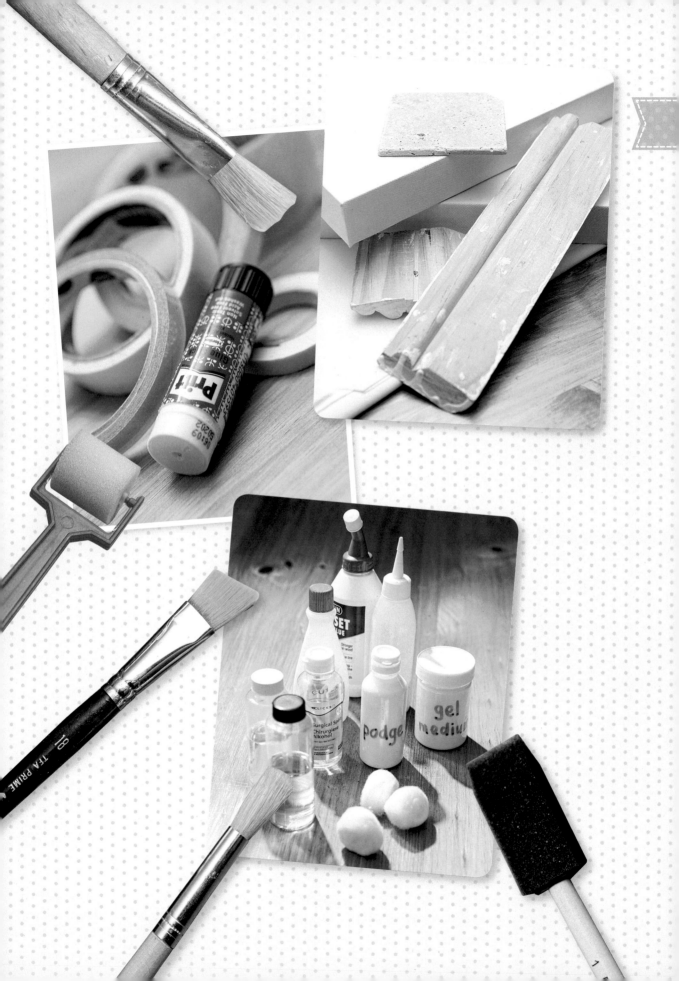

MEDIUMS, MATERIALS AND METHODS

MOD PODGE™ (or podge as I'll refer to it throughout the book): This is a brand name for PVA (Polyvinyl Acetate, the base of white craft glue). It's a multi-purpose, water-based sealer and adhesive that you use to transfer images using the decoupage method. For best results, use photocopies and laser prints printed on standard copier paper. Coat the surface of your project with a thin layer of podge, then 'glue' the image to the surface using more podge. Ensure you remove any trapped air by brushing over any bubbles with a little more pressure, but don't brush over the top of the image repeatedly. This may lift the ink; use your fingers and some gentle pressure instead. When using podge, always replace the lid of the container between applications – the less exposure to air, the longer it will last. Always shake the container before use. Clean your brushes immediately after use with some lukewarm water.

GEL MEDIUM: This is a thick acrylic gel you'll find at craft and hobby shops. Choose a general acrylic gel that is suitable for most crafting purposes. I prefer one with a matte finish. A gel medium is perfect for doing direct transfers onto various surfaces. Photocopy or print your image in reverse onto plain copier paper and trim away any excess paper. Apply a heavy coat of transfer medium onto your surface and a thin coat over the top of your image. Position the image face down onto the surface, taking care not to get any gel medium on the back of the image. Use your fingers to burnish your image to the surface and allow to dry overnight. Don't be worried if it looks slightly lumpy or uneven, as it will not be visible once the paper is removed. Once dry, spray the back of the image with some water, allow to soak and then, using your fingers, gently rub over the paper. Work in circular movements and watch as the paper starts coming off. Be aware that this is a timely process that needs repeated

wetting and more rubbing of the paper until only the ink remains. The end result is going to be well worth the effort, so keep at it!

TRANSFER GLAZE: This is highly adhesive and elastic acrylic glaze that has been specifically designed to transform paper images into thin, flexible plastic transfers, ideal for creating decals. Make a laser print of your image and tape it down onto a glass surface with sticky tape. Coat the top of your image with one thin layer of transfer glaze, running in a horizontal direction. Allow to dry and then follow with a second coat running in a vertical direction. Repeat these steps for coats three and four. Once completely dry, soak the image in a shallow bowl filled with water. Rub the paper backing until it comes off and remove any remaining residue with a soft cloth. Let the decal dry and then affix the image to a surface using a decoupage medium. This is ideal for glass projects as it will allow light to show through and also for curved surfaces as the image will be flexible.

IRON-ON TRANSFER PAPERS: These sheets of paper are made specifically for transferring images to fabrics. Make sure that you use the correct type of paper as some are suited for dark fabrics and others for light fabrics. Don't forget to flip your images before printing when using papers for light coloured materials. Always print a test sheet first to ensure that you are happy with the colouration and size. Also check that you insert the transfer paper into your printer so that it prints on the correct side of the transfer paper. When ironing the image onto your fabric, be sure to use a hard surface such as glass or Formica because it holds the heat. Ironing boards tend to disperse the heat, which results in a less than perfect print. Allow the transfer to cool properly before peeling away the film.

VARNISH: This is a protective coating applied over a finished project. Varnishes are available in water-based or oil-based varieties, as well as gloss or matte finishes. The type you use will depend on the project. For example, canvasses will make do with a basic water-based decoupage varnish but ceramics, with a higher usage rate, will require a polymer varnish.

POLYMER GLOSS: This is composed of two liquids, a resin and a hardener, which when mixed together, harden to form a strong bond. It's ideal for creating a glass-like finish on projects. Make sure to follow the manufacturer's instructions step by step, in a well-ventilated area. To avoid bubbles forming, do not over- or vigorously mix the two compounds. Should bubbles form, simply blow at them through a straw. This gloss requires no less than 24 hours of drying time.

CANVAS: I use artist's canvas bought at craft, hobby or even certain stationery shops. The ideal canvas is stretched tightly across the wooden frame and has a primed finish. When canvasses are on sale, buy plenty and keep them for future use.

MDF (MEDIUM DENSITY FIBERBOARD): This is locally known as hardboard. Basically it is sawdust and glue, fused together under pressure and heat. It is very versatile for decorative projects as it can be found in various sizes and thicknesses and can be cut to almost any shape. The smooth surface is perfect for painting but the edges can be fuzzy. You can smooth the edges by lightly sanding it and wiping away the dust with a damp cloth.

WOOD: This is very easy to handle when working with smaller projects but can be trickier as the projects get bigger. When purchasing lengths of wood for larger projects, make sure that the wood is not warped. Wood warping is the result of uneven drying of lumber. You also need to make sure that your wood has been treated. This basically creates resistance against insects or fungus. If you decide to use the project outdoors, be sure to varnish the wood to avoid water or sun damage. Note that this may need to be done more than once to ensure longevity.

BURNISHING: This is the process during which you transfer an image to a surface by means of pressure. An ideal burnishing tool would be a bone-folder or the back of a spoon.

CRAFT KNIFE: When using a craft knife, make sure the blade is very sharp; if it feels blunt, simply snap off the blunt section. Always use your craft knife in conjunction with a self-healing cutting mat to avoid damaging surfaces. When cutting around an image using a ruler, never place your ruler next to the image. This is to avoid your craft knife slipping and cutting into the image. Rather place your ruler on top of the image and then cut down the sides.

DECOUPAGE: This is the process of applying an image to a surface using a product such as podge and a brush of some sort. When using a delicate paper such as tissue paper, use a soft, flat synthetic brush so as not to damage the paper. To decoupage copier prints onto canvas, use a wider, hard-bristled brush as you'll need more pressure for the thicker paper. For smooth surfaces such as ceramics, a foam applicator is ideal.

PRINTING ON TISSUE PAPER: Unfortunately, tissue paper is too thin to feed through a printer. But there is an easy way to overcome this. Place a sheet of standard A4 (US Letter) copier paper onto the shiny side of the tissue paper. Check whether the printer feeds the paper through the printer in an upright or sideways position. This will determine where you need to fold your tissue paper over the copier paper. Trim the sides of the tissue paper to the size of your A4 (US Letter) printer paper but allow an extra 1cm (½in) at the top and bottom if the printer feeds the paper upright, or allow 1cm (½in) on each side if it feeds the paper sideways. Now fold the 1cm (½in) tissue paper overhang over the copier paper and tape it down using sticky tape. Place your specially created paper into the printer, making sure it's the right way round so that it will print on to the side where the tissue paper is. Now print your picture and stand by while it prints to ensure that the paper feeds through the printer properly. Once the print is dry, separate the tissue paper and apply to your surface with a soft brush.

IDEAS WITH CANVAS

The photo-canvas trend has been around for quite some time, and with good reason. What a beautiful way to display your most cherished memories. In this section I'll show you how to create your own photo canvas with a creative flair that will make your prints one of a kind. There are various techniques you can use so try to pair your image with the technique that best suits the feel of the photo.

Vintage-style canvas

Create an old-world feel by printing on tissue paper and decorating the canvas with classic lace and beautiful paper creations. Because the tissue paper is so thin, the texture of the canvas will still be visible, giving the photograph a very authentic look and feel, almost as though it's been printed directly onto the canvas.

WHAT YOU'LL NEED

Canvas

Prepared sheet of white tissue paper (see instructions on p15)

Laser printer

Craft knife and ruler

Cutting mat

Podge

Foam applicator

Decorations

Useful tip: To create a very smooth finish with no lines or bubbles, place the tissue paper covered canvas face down on a table. Then rub the back of the canvas with a cloth.

1. Print your image to fit your canvas. I chose a sepia print to add to the vintage look I wanted to create.

2. Separate the tissue paper from the copier paper by cutting around the printed area with your craft knife, taking care not to tear the tissue paper.

3. Cover your canvas with a very thin layer of podge using the foam applicator. Place your tissue paper onto the canvas with the printed side facing up, making sure that the sides match up with the canvas. Using your fingers and small circular motions, work from one side to the other to apply your picture to your canvas. Trim off any excess on the sides and make sure to glue them down underneath. Take care not to get any podge on the top of your print.

4. Once dry, embellish your canvas with some classic lace, vintage scrapbook bits or beautiful lettering.

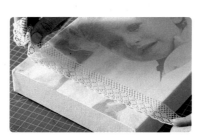

Black and white photo canvas

Photos canvases are easy, fast and very cost-effective to make. They're also a great alternative to grouping a bunch of frames together. Alternate the photos with beautiful quotes that match the images. Black and white photographs are perfect for this type of project as you don't have to worry about colours that might clash.

WHAT YOU'LL NEED

Canvas in various sizes

Black and white laser prints

Craft knife and ruler

Cutting mat

Podge

Paintbrush

Soft cloth

1. Group each print with a canvas and cut the image to size using your craft knife and ruler. Position each picture on top of its corresponding canvas and check that it fits and there is no overhang. Simply trim any excess paper.

2. The images can now be applied to the canvas. Take one canvas and give it a medium coating of podge making sure to cover the top and about 3mm (⅛in) down each side. Take the corresponding picture and paint a thin layer of podge on the back of the print, making sure not to get any medium on the front.

3. Quickly flip the picture over and position it onto the canvas. Smooth the image down using a soft cloth. Massage the picture onto the canvas by making small circular motions on top of the image. Ensure that there are no obvious bubbles by holding the canvas up at an angle and checking it against the light.

4. Apply the first coat of podge over the top of the image in a horizontal direction. Also coat the sides of the canvas with podge.

5. Once the first layer of podge has dried, apply your second coat in vertical strokes.

6. Allow to dry and then coat the canvas with decoupage medium if you so desire.

Distressed canvas

This is a great way to transfer old photos or landscape imagery. The technique adds to the rustic feel of the pictures and creates an almost worn finish. Choose images of vintage cars; old, rusty keys, or a barnyard door with paint that is peeling. Because the image will be transferred face down, remember to flip the image or ask for the image to be mirrored before printing. Be aware that some of the ink from the image will lift as you remove the paper backing but this is ideal to add to that informal look. The lifting of the ink is especially beautiful around the edges of the canvas.

WHAT YOU'LL NEED

Canvas

Laser printed image

Ruler

Craft knife and ruler

Cutting mat

Gel medium

Paintbrush

Small spray bottle filled with water

Dishcloth

Good idea: Find beautiful vintage images online at free resources such as The Graphics Fairy. Alternatively create a vintage or distressed feel by using a photo-editing programme.

1. Trim your laser printed images to fit your canvas using your craft knife, ruler and cutting mat.

2. Cover the top of your canvas with a medium coat of gel and press your picture face down onto the canvas. Rub the back of the picture to secure it into place and try to remove any air bubbles. Set the canvas aside and leave overnight to dry.

3. Once dry, spritz the back of the paper with water so that it is wet all over. You can also wet your dishcloth and place the damp cloth across your canvas. Allow the paper to soak up a bit of the moisture.

4. Using your finger (and a lot of patience) rub the back of the paper in small circular motions until white bits of paper start coming off. Do not rub too hard as you may remove all of the ink. Once the paper starts coming off quite easily, be careful not to use too much water as this may soak through the canvas and cause the wooden frame to warp.

5. Allow to dry for a bit as the remaining white paper will then show more easily. Repeat the above step until there is no more remaining white paper or patches.

6. Finally coat the top and sides of the canvas with the gel for protection, or rub the sides with a clear furniture wax.

Useful tip: You can use sandpaper to give the edges of the canvas an even more distressed look and feel.

Mixed-media collage canvas

Create surface texture on your canvas before layering your images using various techniques. When choosing your pictures, opt for images of the same event, such as a trip abroad or a birthday party and group the canvasses together so that they tell a story. If you're going to use a gel medium and the reverse application technique, flip all images and text before printing.

WHAT YOU'LL NEED

Canvas

Grey craft paint

White acrylic PVA

White ready-mixed crack filler

Old brush

Plastic cake stencil or similar items to create pattern

Laser printer

Craft knife

Gel medium

Paintbrush

Podge

Decorative elements

Gold leaf

Gold size

Soft paintbrush

Useful tips: Find non-copyrighted graphics and images from free websites such as vintagefeedsacks. blogspot.com or graphicsfairy.com.

When using size, use cheap disposable brushes or try cleaning the brush with acetone.

1. Coat the top of your canvas with a base coat of grey craft paint and allow to dry. You can of course use another paint colour better suited to the theme of your images.

2. Mix equal parts of white acrylic paint to the ready-mixed crack filler. Make sure to mix it well to avoid any clumping. Paint a thick layer over the top of each canvas and set aside for one hour.

3. After one hour, take your cake stencil and press it onto the still slightly wet paint and grout mixture. Press down on all the plastic areas to really create a three-dimensional pattern in the paint. Lift up and repeat on different areas, such as the corners of the canvas. Once done the canvas must be left to dry completely.

4. Whilst waiting you can prepare your photos. Size your images to various sizes to fit inside the shape of your canvas. Play around with bigger and smaller options and rather print more images so you can layer them over each other. Also include some appropriate graphics and text. Print onto standard copier paper and then cut out each individual image.

5. Apply non-reversed images with podge and a paintbrush using the basic decoupage technique. Once that is dry you can overlay these images with your reversed images and text. Use a gel medium for this technique and apply the image upsidedown. Create a nice layering effect by overlapping podge and gel medium pictures. Once the gel medium has dried overnight, wet and rub off with your fingertips.

6. Finally you can embellish your canvasses with 3D elements and gold leaf. To apply the gold leaf, brush a small amount onto the desired area. Allow to become tacky and then place a piece of gold leaf over it. Leave for a few minutes and then use a clean brush to brush away the excess gold leaf.

Christening gift

Before sending your images to print, add some text to your design by using simple text boxes in software programmes such as Microsoft Word or Paint. Finally embellish the canvas with some creative cutouts. This is ideal as a personalized gift.

WHAT YOU'LL NEED

4 square primed canvasses
(15cm x 15cm/6in x 6in)

4 laser printed images
with text added

Scrapbook papers and offcuts

Craft knife and ruler

Podge

Brush

Cloth

Varnish

1. Print your images slightly bigger than your canvas size to allow for inconsistencies in the canvas.

2. Cut the images to size according to each canvas and then cut out some creative shapes from your scrapbook papers to compliment the design of each print. Lay these out next to each other to get a better idea of the balance of the design. Take a quick snapshot with your cellphone or digital camera as reference for later.

3. Coat the first canvas with podge, taking care to also cover the sides. Also coat the back of your image with a thin layer of podge. Quickly flip it over onto the canvas, making sure not to get any podge on the front of the image. Place your first image face up on the canvas and smooth down using your fingers or a cloth. Once you are happy, coat the entire image and sides with podge. Repeat this process with all four canvasses.

4. Once the podge has dried, start arranging your scrapbook cutouts on the canvasses and then glue them into place using podge. Coat the top of the scrapbook items to give an overall glossy finish.

5. Once dry, you can coat all the canvasses with a decoupage varnish to act as protection.

Een plus een is gelyk aan twee
'n mega en giga bite
maak my ook nie meer verleë
maar om ouer te raak
vra veel meer
as om snags te waak

Albert Gideon Butler
het ons lewens kom vul
Ons voel regtig soos 'n nul
Hoe wat en waar
Net om die kind
te laat bedaar

Al weet ons dalk min
Ons sal hom
tot die dood bemin
Aan u Here
sê ons dankie
Vir elke klankie
en ja ook vir elke stankie

Ons gaan hom
aan die Here wy
En ons hoop u is ook daarby
Sondag 29 Augustus
so die Here wil
Waar anders
as op Leipoldtville.

albert gideon butler
gebore
8 Junie 2

IDEAS WITH HARDBOARD

The great thing about hardboard is that it's much cheaper than wood and craft shops stock a great variety of ready-made items, from coasters to jewellery boxes, that you can simply buy and decorate to your heart's desire. The only downside to hardboard is that because it's quite porous, it needs to be handled with care and does not react well to water. But other than that it's a really fun and versatile medium that can really make you stretch your imagination and creativity.

Spotted giraffe

This is a fun idea for a child's room. If you struggle to find the right hardboard cutout, simply have one cut. This is a really fun idea for a child's room. When painting the cutout, make sure you choose a colour that will match the rest of the decor in the room.

WHAT YOU'LL NEED

6mm (¼in) hardwood cutout in silhouette shape of a giraffe

Pastel yellow acrylic paint

Paintbrush

Podge

Laser copies of your photos

Circle stencil

Pencil

Paintbrush with soft bristles

Scissors

Craft knife

Useful tip: If you do not have a circular stencil, simply turn shot glasses upside down and trace around the rim with a pencil.

1. Wipe the surface of the cutout to remove any dust. Coat the entire top and sides with two layers of acrylic paint.

2. While the paint is drying, prepare your images. Take your laser copies and trace circular shapes on top of the copies using your pencil and stencil. Look for interesting areas within the image such as a hand or a close-up of a smile. Once done, cut out all of your circular shapes.

3. Roughly position all your circular cutouts on the giraffe. Using your soft bristle brush and podge, glue the images into place by coating the bottom of the circle and then placing it on the giraffe. Cover the top of the each circle with a layer of podge – smoothing out any bubbles. Repeat with all of your laser copy cutouts until you are happy with the outcome.

4. Once the podge has dried, flip the giraffe over onto your cutting mat. Use your craft knife to trim off any excess paper sticking out over the sides.

5. Cover the entire top and sides of the cutout with a layer of podge.

Antique jewellery box

Transform an everyday hardboard box into a beautiful treasure trove in which to keep your jewellery. Give the modern feel of the hardboard box a vintage look using distressed paint effects. I used wood glue instead of an antique crackle medium, which can be quite expensive.

WHAT YOU'LL NEED

Hardwood jewellery box

White matte acrylic paint

Clear drying white wood or craft glue

Paintbrush with rough bristles

Paintbrush with soft bristles

Gold acrylic paint

Gloss printed photograph

Craft knife and ruler

Superglue

High-gloss polymer coating

Old plastic account card

Useful tip: For an easier application, unscrew the clip and hinges before painting the box. Reattach once the paint is completely dry.

1. Wipe your jewellery box with a soft cloth to remove any dust. Coat the entire box with two coats of the white acrylic paint, allowing the paint to dry between coats.

2. Using a thick bristled brush apply a medium coat of glue all over the sides of the box. Work fast and ensure even coverage.

3. When the glue is almost dry but still tacky, take your finer brush and paint a thick coat of gold acrylic paint over the glue. Allow the gold paint to dry and you will see cracks appearing all over. Note that the thicker your glue the bigger the cracks and vice versa. Also paint the top of the lid with gold paint.

4. While the box is drying, prepare your photo. Cut it to fit the top of the jewellery box. I prefer leaving a small edge of gold showing around the image. Using superglue, glue your photo to the top of the box making sure you coat up to the edge of the photo and smooth the image down using your fingers. Allow to dry while you prepare your polymer coating.

5. Mix your polymer coating according to the manufacturer's instructions and pour it onto the centre of the image. Ensure your jewellery box is positioned on a flat, level surface. Pour a bit of the polymer mix onto the centre of your image. Using the plastic card, force your polymer to the edges the box, taking care not to have it run over the sides. Cover the entire top of the box and remember that the polymer mix is self-levelling so don't worry to get a perfectly smooth finish. Allow to dry completely in an area where no dust will settle on it.

Six-sided cube puzzle

This is not only a quirky way to display photographs but also a fun educational toy for children. Ideal as a gift for a child's birthday or just something with which to keep a very busy toddler entertained.

WHAT YOU'LL NEED

12 hardboard cutouts
(8cm x 8cm x 9mm/3¼in x 3¼in
x ⅜in)

12 hardboard cutouts
(8cm x 6.2cm x 9mm/3¼in x
2⅜in x ⅜in)

12 hardboard cutouts
(6.2cm x 6cm x 9mm/2⅜in x 2⅜in
x ⅜in)

Nail gun

Strong wood adhesive

Paintbrush

6 A3 (US Ledger) laser copies
of your photos (images to be
printed no smaller than 24cm x
16cm/9½in x 6¼in)

Craft knife

Cutting mat

Ruler

Pencil

Podge

Decoupage varnish

1. Construct your six hardwood cubes. Combine two of each size to create the six sides of the cube. Using the nail gun and wood adhesive, construct your six cubes one by one. Once the cubes are completed, wipe them with a damp cloth to remove any hardwood residue.

2. Cut each photo to the combined size of six cubes which is 24cm x 16cm (9½in x 6¼in). Now flip the image over and draw the six 8cm x 8cm (3¼in x 3¼in) blocks on the back. Carefully cut out using your craft knife and cutting mat.

3. Lay your cubes down in two rows with three blocks in each row. Position your picture cutouts close by and start applying the images to the cubes. Coat the hardwood with podge, position your picture on top of the podge. Once you are happy, brush over the top of the picture with more podge. To ensure a smooth coverage with no bubbles, smooth over the podge with your finger whilst it is still wet. Repeat this process with all six cubes.

4. Once the images have dried, flip each cube over so that the image is facedown on the cutting mat. Using a very sharp craft knife, trim any excess paper edges.

5. Repeat steps 3 and 4 on the other five sides of your cubes. Once all the cubes are completely covered and dry, coat each cube with decoupage varnish.

Great tip: If making these cubes yourself seems a little daunting, have them made at your local DIY store.

Memory box

Make your special holiday moments last longer by displaying photos in a memory box. Collect trinkets such as ticket stubs, shells and coins during your travels and add that to the display to make it really tell the whole story.

WHAT YOU'LL NEED

1.5cm (⅝in) hardboard box
(25cm x 25cm/10in x 10in)

Craft paint

Paintbrush

Scrapbook paper to suit
the theme

Craft knife

Glue stick

10cm x 15cm (4in x 6in) gloss
photos with a white border

Trinkets from your trip

Superglue

1. Wipe the inside of the box with a damp cloth to remove any dust. Coat the entire box with craft paint in your chosen colour until the coverage is even and solid.

2. Cut your scrapbook paper to fit inside the bottom of the box and paste into place using the glue stick.

3. Arrange your photos and trinkets inside the box so that they create a balanced overall look. Glue into place using superglue and allow for the glue to dry completely before lifting up the box to admire your handiwork.

Good idea: When displaying various memory boxes of different events on the same wall, keep the colour of the boxes the same to create a more cohesive look.

It's a sign

Beautiful hardwood cutouts and wording are easy to come by at just about any craft or DIY shop. If you can't find exactly what you're looking for, simply pop over to your local laser-cutting store and ask them to create it for you. Take care when positioning your images, making sure you don't cut off any important or defining parts.

WHAT YOU'LL NEED

Hardboard cutout

Laser print

Sticky tape

Pencil

Podge

Brush

Craft knife and cutting mat

1. Measure your hardboard cutout and have your image printed a few centimetres or inches bigger than the cutout. This is to ensure that you have more flexibility to move the image around until you find the perfect position.

2. Stick your laser print up against a window with some tape, making sure that the printed side faces away from you. Ensure that there is sufficient sunlight streaming through the window as this will act as a makeshift light box. Using the sunlight as a guide, move your cutout over the back of the image to a position where the image best fits the cutout. Once you are happy, trace around the cutout using a pencil. You will now have a pencil outline on the back of your image to act as a guide when pasting down your cutout.

3. Lay your image facedown on a flat surface. Coat the front of your hardboard cutout with a layer of podge and then position it onto the pencil outline. Flip the cutout over and smooth down the paper using a soft cloth, removing any bubbles in the process. Allow to dry.

4. Finally place the cutout facedown onto a cutting mat. Using a very sharp craft knife, cut off the excess paper sticking out over the sides. Coat the top of the image with a layer of podge.

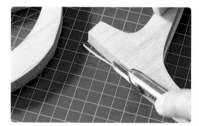

Hearts delight

Display beautiful close-ups of interesting surfaces or textures on hardboard hearts. Hang them as they are, or decorate it further with other embellishments like a miniature vase.

WHAT YOU'LL NEED

Hardboard heart cutout

Drill

Off-white craft paint

Paintbrush

Sandpaper

Black and white mirror printed laser image

Craft knife and cutting mat

Gel medium

Spray bottle filled with water

Miniature glass vase

10cm (4in) of wire (0.9mm/$^1/_{32}$in)

Wooden beads and twine

1. Drill a small hole in the top of the heart where the twine will go through, and another small hole for the wire that will hold the miniature vase in place. Coat the top of the heart with a layer of off-white paint. Once dry, sand the edges of the heart to create a semi-distressed look.

2. Lay your print face up and place your cutout the wrong way round over the print; trim around the edges using your craft knife.

3. Coat the top of the heart with a layer of gel medium and lay the image face down onto the surface. Smooth it down using your fingers or a cloth, making sure not to get any of the gel medium on the back of the print. Allow to dry overnight.

4. Spray the back of the image with water and allow to soak. Using your fingertips, rub over the back of the paper until the paper starts coming off. Repeat this process, saturating the paper as needed until all of it is removed.

5. Attach your vase to the heart by looping the wire around the neck of the vase and then sticking the two wire ends through the hole in the centre of the heart. At the back of the heart, twist the ends of the wire together and then fold it flat so that it won't slip through.

6. Push your twine through the top hole and tie into a knot. Thread your beads onto each piece of twine and tie a knot again at the top.

IDEAS WITH WOOD

There's something about wood that makes me feel rather nostalgic. With its beautiful grain and rough texture, it's really a masterpiece from nature. That's why when working with wood, I like to showcase some of those features and really celebrate the natural characteristics of the wood. It's also is an ideal medium because it is so durable and really lends itself to a giving your project a real feel of quality.

Ideally, when deciding to work with wood, try and find leftover pieces of timber. Alternatively, repurpose an old piece of wood or furniture. It can be anything from an old cabinet door to offcuts of wood lying around the garage. Recycling old wood can really add to the character and give even more depth and meaning to the project.

Tree branch frame

Make this frame in no time at all, with minimum effort and at almost no expense.

WHAT YOU'LL NEED

A4 (US Letter) sheet of clear hard plastic (found at stationery shops)

Craft knife and ruler

Old branch

Handsaw

Staple gun

20cm (8in) decorative ribbon

10cm x 15cm (4in x 6in) gloss photo

1. Cut your A4 (US Letter) sheet of plastic into two 17cm x 10cm (6¼in x 4in) pieces.

2. Saw two 10cm (4in) long pieces from the branch, trying to use interesting areas of the wood.

3. Line up your two pieces of plastic and staple it onto the two branch pieces at the top and bottom. Staple the left and right corners of the branch to ensure that it's secure.

4. Staple the ribbon to the back so that it creates a loop for the frame to hang from.

5. Slide your picture between the two pieces of plastic. If the image doesn't slide in easily, simply trim it a little.

Good idea: You can also use drift wood or painted dowel sticks instead of tree branches.

Wood print

The most striking aspect of this project is the beautiful wood grain and how it adds to the character of the picture. Choose a photograph that will complement the natural look of the wood. Edit this image to black and white, and add some distressing effects if you feel it needs it. You can also up the contrast and brightness of the images with an image-editing programme.

WHAT YOU'LL NEED

2.1cm (¾ in) pine (2 pieces of 55cm x 40cm/20in x 15¾in)

2.1cm pine (2 pieces of 55cm x 35.8cm/20in x 13¾in)

2.1cm pine (1 piece of 35.8cm x 35.8cm/13¾in x 13¾in)

Nail gun

Wood glue

2 black and white mirrored laser prints (55cm x 40cm/20in x 15¾in)

Acrylic gel medium

Paintbrush

Old towel

Spray bottle filled with water

Dry cloth

Sandpaper

Varnish

Good idea: You can treat the wood with a colour stain before covering it with wax.

1. Construct the pine "table" using your nail gun and wood glue. The final result will be a box with four sides and a top.

2. Cut both images to size.

3. Coat one 55cm x 40cm (20in x 15¾in) side of wood with an even layer of gel ensuring than it's not too thin but that you do not end up with blobs of gel.

4. Now place the print facedown on to the wood and smooth it down all over without moving the image. Try and remove any air bubbles by smoothing them over with a hard item such as a pencil or a ruler. Allow for it to dry overnight without touching it.

5. Wet the towel to the point where it is soaked, but not dripping. Place the towel on top of the laser print. This will get the paper to start softening. Remove the towel and with circular motions start removing the paper with your fingers. This is a time consuming task and needs to be done with caution to ensure you don't rub off the ink at the bottom. If the paper starts to dry out, wet it again using your spray bottle and repeat the process of removing the remaining paper. Do this until all white remnants of the paper have been removed.

6. Repeat steps 3 to 5 on the opposite side of the box.

7. Once all the paper has been removed, wipe clean with a dry cloth to remove any fibrous residue left over by the paper. Gently sand the edges of the wood to remove any excess gel. Coat the entire surface with a layer of wood varnish (or you can use furniture wax if you don't wish to change the colour of the wood).

Skirting around

Skirting board offcuts are something that can be found at various building sites, if you are lucky enough to find a friendly foreman to help you! The more variety of shapes you can find, the better the end result. Combine these various shapes with photographs that tell a similar story in order to tie it all together.

WHAT YOU'LL NEED

Skirting board offcuts

Sandpaper and wood filler

Damp cloth

2 paint colours of your choice

Paintbrush

Matt photos

Craft knife and ruler

220 grit sandpaper

Scrapbook letters

Craft glue

Paintbrush

1. Prepare the surface of the skirting board. Sand the wood to a smooth finish with sandpaper. Remove any rough spots or inconsistencies on the surface by filling in dents with wood filler and then sanding smooth. Finally wipe the surface of the wood clean with a damp cloth.

2. Apply your first coat of paint to the top and sides of the skirting boards. Note that this will be your base coat and will show when we distress the wood. Once dry apply your second colour over the side and top.

3. While the paint from the second coat dries you can prepare your photographs. Cut each photo to fit onto the flat area of a skirting board piece.

4. When the paint is dry take a piece of sandpaper and distress the wood where you feel appropriate.

5. Glue on your images and scrapbook letters with craft glue and a brush.

Good idea: Create small frames from leftover skirting board pieces by simply cutting the edges at a 45 degree angle and stapling together using a staple gun.

Portrait photos: Charlene Schreuder

Explore a door

Ever wondered what to do with that old and worn cupboard door? Let me show you!

WHAT YOU'LL NEED

Old cupboard doors (cleaned well and doorknobs removed)

Tissue paper

Pencil

Large scale laser prints

Craft knife or scissors

Spray adhesive

Decoupage varnish

1. Measure the inside of your doorframes where the images will go. The easiest way to achieve the correct shape and size is to layer a piece of tissue paper over the door and press it into the corners and then trace with a pencil. Size your images to the approximate area they need to cover and print.

2. Using your tissue paper as a template, trace the outline onto your printed images and cut out. Glue the images onto the doors using a thin layer spray adhesive, which you apply to the back of the prints. Smooth onto the wood using a soft cloth.

3. You can coat your images with a layer of decoupage varnish or leave as they are if you do not want a glossy finish.

4. Finally, rescrew the old doorknobs or add new decorative doorknobs as I have.

Useful tip: You can find ideal surfaces such as old trays, doors, and window frames at local flea markets for really good prices. Don't be afraid to bargain either!

Wordy wooden cutouts

As the saying goes, a picture says a thousand words or in this case – three! Create fun cutouts with your existing photographs and display them on painted pieces of wood.

WHAT YOU'LL NEED

3 pieces of pine
(22cm x 10.5cm/8½in x 4in)

Blue enamel paint

White enamel paint

Tile scraper

Electric drill

7mm (5/16in) drill bit (size to fit thickness of rope)

3 jumbo matt photos (no borders)

Inkjet printouts of bold words that suit the images

Craft knife

Scissors

Pencil

Podge

Paintbrush

Decoupage varnish

7mm (5/16in) thick natural fibre rope

1. Coat the top and sides of each piece of wood with blue enamel paint. Allow to dry and then repeat with the white enamel.

2. Once dry use your tile scraper to knock, dent and scrape at the paint to create a distressed look. Scrape horizontally and vertically to get the desired effect. Try to scrape deep enough so that some of the wood at the bottom also shows.

3. Drill a hole into each corner per wooden panel.

4. Now you can prepare your images. Layer a word over a photo, flip over and hold up against a window. Using the sun as a light box, position the word and photo until you are happy that the image fills the word appropriately.

5. Using your pencil, trace the word onto the back of the photo. Repeat with all three photos and then cut out the letters using your craft knife and scissors.

6. Position each word onto a piece of wood and glue into place using podge. When all the words are done and the podge has dried, coat all three pieces with decoupage varnish.

7. Finally thread your rope through the holes, tie a knot at the bottom and display.

Useful tip: When drilling the holes ensure they are not too big. Otherwise your rope will simply slip through and not hold the wooden pieces in place. To make the rope easier to thread through – wrap sticky tape tightly around each end of the rope and remove afterwards.

Balsa wood silhouettes

Balsa wood is a very thin sheet of wood used by model builders. It comes in various thicknesses and is ideal because it can cut using only a craft knife. In this project I combined wooden frames with balsa wood silhouette cutouts to create interesting shapes for your prized photos to show through.

WHAT YOU'LL NEED

Beach wood frames

Balsa wood
(no thicker than 1mm/$^{1}/_{32}$in)

Craft knife

Pencil

Carbon paper

Ruler

Inkjet printouts of
silhouette shapes

Gloss photos to fit frames

Masking tape

1. Remove the glass from the frames and trace the glass outlines onto the flat piece of balsa wood. Cut out each panel using a craft knife.

2. Trace your silhouettes onto the pieces of balsa wood using carbon paper and cut out each shape. Take care that the craft knife does not slip and damage the remaining balsa wood.

3. Position a photo behind each piece of balsa wood and once you are happy with it tape it to the back and trim off any excess photo sticking out over the sides.

4. Pop the balsa wood cutouts back into each frame and display.

Useful tip: If your balsa wood strip is not wide enough simply join two pieces with a piece of tape at the back. Check to see that the wood grain on the front is somewhat similar.

IDEAS WITH GLASS

Glass is ideal for craft projects as it is readily available, durable and very versatile. Most importantly, by repurposing glass we are encouraging a greener environment!

Vintage bottle display

Old glass bottles make beautiful display vessels for photographs, especially if you choose photos with a vintage feel to them. Try black and white or sepia. For a more modern take, place colourful pictures in upside down jam and food jars.

WHAT YOU'LL NEED

Old glass bottles (glass must still be semi clear)

Old photos

Craft knife and ruler

Long thin utensil (such as back of a paintbrush or thin screwdriver)

1. Arrange your bottles in a row and try to match each one up with a photo that will best fit the inside of the bottle. If a photo is too long or wide, simply cut it slightly smaller. For a nice big round bottle you can use an elongated photo that can go right around the inside of the bottle.

2. Gently bend each picture so that it will fit through the neck of the bottle.

3. For bottles with very small necks, roll the picture to a size that will fit and then squeeze it into the bottle and let it drop in. Don't worry if the picture stays curled up, simply use your long tool to press the picture down by applying pressure to the centre of the picture. This will force the sides of the picture to "pop" out.

Good idea: Glue one of the photos to the back of one of the taller bottles by using podge. Fill the bottle with water and place a single stem flower in it. This will add some colour and vibrancy to the display.

Olive oil photo bottle

Create a fun housewarming gift by displaying a photo inside a bottle filled with olive oil. Try and use a memory that was shared by you and the recipient. Perhaps a photo taken of the both of you or a beautiful scenic shot of a trip shared abroad or locally. Remember to inform the recipient that this gift is for display only, not for consumption.

WHAT YOU'LL NEED

Tall bottle with cap or cork

Photo to fit inside bottle (paper copies of photos won't work)

Tweezers or thin tongs

Olive oil (non-flavoured)

Small card and ribbon

1. Insert the picture into the bottle, using tweezers or tongs to hold it in place if needs be.

2. Gently pour the olive oil into the jar. Once full you can let go of the photo and it should stay in place.

3. Secure the cap and tie a pretty ribbon with card around the bottle neck.

Good idea: Add a sprig of rosemary to the inside before adding the oil to create an authentic Italian feel; chillies will work well for a Mexican feel.

Memory jars

Truly capture a moment in time by combining photos with items taken from the scene. You can get really creative with this project. Perhaps your wedding day, a day at the beach or a birthday party will act as the inspiration. Make sure you keep some bits from the event and similarly themed craft items to enhance the theme.

WHAT YOU'LL NEED

Glass mason jars with lids

Laser printouts of photos to fit inside the jar

Memorabilia from that moment

Embellishments

Scrapbook paper to suit the theme

Scissors

Craft glue

Cardboard

Ribbon

1. Ensure that your jars are clean and dry on the inside.

2. Fill the bottom of the jars with something to suit the theme of the photo. For example, sand, faux grass, colourful beads, leaves or dried flowers.

3. Position the photos inside the jar by having it lean against the glass.

4. Fill the rest of the jar with small trinkets from the day or adornments that suit the theme

5. Once you are happy with the inside, cut a piece of scrapbook paper to fit the top of the lid and glue into place.

6. Print out a special note from that day and glue it onto a card. Cut the card into a decorative tag and attach to the bottle using a pretty ribbon.

Good idea: Create a memory jar for each birthday of a child and arrange them on a shelf in chronological order.

See-through vase

Applying images to a vase can be tricky because of its curved shape. Using the technique below, however, it's child's play and you'll soon have a beautiful see-through image.

WHAT YOU'LL NEED

Black and white laser printout with clear outlines (in order to cut around)

Transfer glaze

Foam applicator

Scissors

Podge

Paintbrush

Glass vase (clear or tinted)

Small paintbrush

Polyurethane varnish

1. Apply a horizontal coating of the transfer glaze over your picture with the foam applicator. Allow to dry and then go over it with a second, vertical coat of glaze. Once dry, give it a third and final coat.

2. Once the third coat of glaze has dried cut around the image using your scissors.

3. Hold the image under running water and start rubbing at the paper backing until it comes off. Carry on doing this until all the paper fibres are removed. Lay the image gloss side down and allow to dry.

4. Coat the back of the image with a layer of podge and then quickly place the image onto the vase. Secure it into position using your fingers and brush, making sure to remove any air bubbles. Wipe away any excess podge around the image using a cotton bud and tissues.

5. Once dry you can coat the entire vase with polyurethane varnish if you are concerned that it may get submerged in water for long periods of time.

Crystal photo pendant

Display your cherished photographs of loved ones in an accessory that can be worn and enjoyed.

WHAT YOU'LL NEED

Glass crystal bead with one side that is flat

Laser copy of photo

Craft knife

Podge

Brush

Clear polyurethane varnish

Decorative clip and chain

1. Glue your image to the flat side of the glass crystal using your brush and podge. Also paint the back of the image and smooth out any air bubbles by rubbing over the wet podge with your finger. Allow to dry.

2. Using a very sharp craft knife, cut off the excess paper sticking out around the edges of the bead. Once trimmed, coat the edges and back of the bead with clear polyurethane varnish and leave until completely dry.

3. Poke a needle through the hole in the crystal in order to pierce the paper image and then attach your clip. Slip a pretty chain through it and it's ready to wear.

Miniature bottle pendant

Make a unique pendant with small photos that can easily be changed every once in a while.

WHAT YOU'LL NEED

Laser copy of photo

Miniature glass bottle with cork topper

Chain hook

Small pliers

Jewel decorations such as beads and ornaments

Chain

1. Photocopy your image but reduce the size of it before printing so that it will fit inside your bottle. Trim your image, roll it up and insert into the bottle.

2. Press the chain hook through the top of the cork. Trim the hook and bend the wire sideways to ensure it does not slide out.

3. Attach the chain and add other decorative beads as you desire.

Good idea: Keep the pendant fresh and fun by changing the image inside every so often.

Glass chopping board

Transform an ordinary chopping board with an appetizing photograph you've taken yourself! Choose a picture that suits the vibe and feel of your kitchen, or choose something that will add colour to a bland work top.

WHAT YOU'LL NEED

Glass cutting board

Laser print

Craft knife

Podge

Foam applicator

Polyurethane varnish

Good idea: Create a glass paperweight by repeating the process as above but instead of using silicone buttons on the bottom, cut a piece of felt and glue it on with craft glue.

1. Ensure that the bottom of your cutting board is clean and grease free. Also remove any silicone non-slip buttons, keep aside and reglue once done.

2. Position your cutting board over your laser print and cut around it using a craft knife.

3. Coat the bottom of your cutting board with a medium layer of podge. Also quickly and gently coat the front of your laser print. Place the laser print facedown onto the cutting board and smooth over the back of the print using your hand. Remove any obvious air trapped between the glass and the image. Coat the entire back of the print with podge and use your fingers to smooth out any remaining bubbles.

4. Allow to dry completely and then trim off any excess paper sticking out around the sides.

5. Finally coat the entire bottom and sides of the cutting board with a polyurethane varnish, which will make it resistant to damage when wiping with a wet cloth.

Quick-fix candle holders

Easy to do, you can make candle holders to suit any theme or colour. Afterwards, simply peel off the tape and the glasses are as good as new.

WHAT YOU'LL NEED

Laser printed images

4.8cm (1¾in) clear packaging tape

Burnishing tool

Craft knife

Ruler

Bowl with water

Various sized glasses or containers

Washi tape

1. Print your laser images onto A4 (US Letter) sheets of standard copier paper.

2. Take strips of packaging tape and stick them down over the top of the laser image. Smooth the tape down using your hand, flip the paper over and vigorously rub over the back of the paper using a burnishing tool.

3. Turn the paper back so that the image faces upwards. Use your craft knife and ruler to cut along the edges of the image, trimming off all the excess paper and tape.

4. Submerge the strips in a bowl of water, not too many at a time, and allow to soak.

5. Once the paper is nice and wet start rubbing at it to remove the paper backing. Continue doing this until there is no more paper residue.

6. Lay the wet strip of tape face (glossy side) down onto a flat surface and allow to dry.

7. Once dried the strips should still have enough glue on the back in order to stick to the glass, if not simply use some podge. Tape your images onto the glass and cut to size if needed.

8. Finally decorate the edges with some fun washi tape.

Good idea: Create a hanging lantern by attaching some wire to the rim of the glass container.

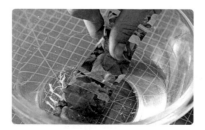

Photos of flowers and greenery: Margaux Tait

IDEAS WITH CERAMICS

Ceramic surfaces can be a little tricky when it comes to the application of images, but with a little trial and error, using various techniques, you'll find your feet in no time. I often find inspiration by simply walking around the house and looking for ceramic items that have long been forgotten. That old set of inherited crockery, surplus tiles or even an ordinary mug that could do with an update. Any one of these items can be transformed into a beautiful piece of decor or a special, handmade gift.

Plate display

Take a trip down Memory Lane and combine beautiful family portraits with heirloom crockery. Group the plates together on a wall or coat with a ceramic medium to use as platters.

WHAT YOU'LL NEED

Various sized plates

Methylated spirits (denatured alcohol) or vinegar

Laser or photocopies of old photographs

Compass

Scissors

Podge

Paintbrush

1. Clean the inside and remove any grease from your plates using methylated spirits (denatured alcohol) or vinegar.

2. Cut your images to fit the insides of the plates using your scissors and a compass. I find circles much easier to cut with a pair of scissors rather than a craft knife.

3. Group each photo and plate together to ease the process of applying the images to the plates. Brush the inside as well as the back of the image with podge, then stick the two together. Gently rub over the top to remove any bubbles.

4. Once all the plates are done, coat all your images with a layer of podge.

Good idea: If your plates are purely ornamental, use original photographs and stick them to the plates with double-sided tape.

Useful tip: You can remove an image from a plate by soaking the plate in warm, soapy water.

Pretty tissue paper plates

Many books show you how to decorate plates using paper napkins and a decoupage technique. But this forces you to use the mass-produced images they print on paper napkins, and I'd much rather decorate my plate with a beautiful close-up image of a flower I took in my very own garden. Here I'll show you step by step how to do this.

WHAT YOU'LL NEED

Glossy white plates

2 sheets of prepared tissue paper

Laser printer

Podge

Scissors

Synthetic fine bristle brush

Oven

1. Make sure the insides of your plates are clean.

2. Print various photos of flowers onto your tissue paper.

3. Cut out the images according to how you'd like them displayed on your plate.

4. Roughly position the cutouts on your plates to ensure that you are happy with the overall balance.

5. Apply the cutouts to the plates by brushing the area with podge and then placing the cutout over it. Carefully brush over the top of the image with more podge, making sure that the tissue paper does not tear.

6. Work quite quickly, covering the entire surface of the plate and the sides where the tissue paper might overlap, with podge.

7. Allow to dry completely and then give a second overall coat in an alternate direction.

8. Once dried, bake in a medium oven according to the manufacturer's instructions with the oven door slightly ajar.

Photographs of flowers: Margaux Tait

Memorable mugs

These mugs are handwashable and a perfect gift for grandma or grandpa. The flexibility of this transfer method makes it easy to use on any curved object.

WHAT YOU'LL NEED

Laser copies of photos

Transfer glaze

Scissors

Glazed ceramic mugs

Podge

Polyurethane varnish

1. Coat your images with three layers of transfer glaze. Remember to allow time to dry between each coat and to do the brushstrokes of each layer in an alternate direction.

2. Once the final coat of glaze has dried, neatly cut out the image.

3. Hold the image underneath running water and remove the paper backing by rubbing it with your fingers. Lay aside to dry with the glossy side facing down.

4. Position your picture on your mug and glue it into place using podge.

5. Once the podge has dried, cover the entire image with polyurethane varnish to ensure that it is washable.

NOTE: It's best to handwash these mugs in warm, soapy water as they're definitely not dishwasher safe.

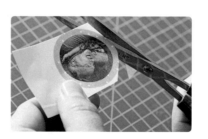

Good idea: Frame your picture with scrapbook paper to provide it with a decorative edge.

Tile coasters

You won't believe how quick and easy it is to make these coasters. The fumes from the varnish remover can be quite strong though, so make sure you work in a well-ventilated area.

WHAT YOU'LL NEED

Mirrored laser copies of your photos

Craft knife and ruler

Unsealed travertine tiles (9.5cm x 9.5cm/3¾in x 3¾in)

Nail polish remover (with acetone)

Cotton wool

Latex gloves to protect your hands (optional)

Tile sealer or varnish

Good idea: Add felt to the bottom of the coasters to stop them from scratching surfaces.

1. Cut your images slightly smaller than the size of the tile to allow for a small border. Round the edges if you prefer.

2. Heat each tile in the microwave for about one minute. This will help the ink transfer to the tile more easily.

3. Place your image face down onto the warm tile and pour some polish remover onto a ball of cotton wool. Rub this over the back of the image until the entire surface of the image is covered with nail polish.

4. Hold the image in place and do not move it about. If the polish remover starts evaporating, simply pour some more onto the cotton wool and rub the image again.

5. Lift one corner of the colour copy to see if the image is transferring. If you're happy with the results, leave to dry for a few minutes.

6. When all the tiles are done, peel off the paper. Remove any paper residue with the tips of your fingers.

7. Lastly, seal with tile sealer or varnish.